BOUNDARIES IN MARRIAGE AND RELATIONSHIPS

How to enjoy long lasting marriage and relationships by being your true self

Dr James Malcom

INTRODUCTION

What is a boundary?

A boundary is a line where you end and others start. Boundaries are the rules that let others realize how to treat you and how you will react on the off chance that somebody stretches those boundaries.

When you think about a boundary, what rings a bell? You may consider something like a property line or the characterizing lines of a shape. Boundary show where one thing closes and another starts. The boundary in a relationship is somewhat similar to this; they help every individual sort out where one thing finishes and another starts. To put it plainly, boundaries assist you with characterizing what you are all right with and how you might want to be treated by others. They apply to any sort of relationship you have, regardless of whether with a companion, relative, partner or any other person in your life. Boundaries are an approach to deal with ourselves.

At the point when we set boundaries, we're less angry on the grounds that our requirements are getting met. Boundaries make our expectations understood, so others realize what's in store for us and how we need to be dealt with. Boundaries are the establishment of good, sound relationships in dating, between friends and marriage.

CHAPTER ONE

SETTING BOUNDARIES

To set up boundaries, you should be clear with your partner what your identity is, the thing that you need, your convictions and values, and your limit points. Defining boundaries for yourself that reflect what your identity is and who you at last need to be will just improve defining boundaries with your partner in a relationship.

Despite the fact that we talk about them according to others, somehow or other boundaries are truly about your relationship with yourself; they help you honor your necessities, objectives, sentiments, and qualities. Boundary can be passionate, physical, or even emotional. A few examples of individual boundaries may be:

• I'm cool with following each other via social media, yet not cool with sharing passwords

• I'm happy with kissing and clasping hands, yet not out in the open where people might see us.

- I'm all right with consistent messaging, however, I would prefer not to message on more than once in 60 minutes

- I need to keep company with my family during the week, so I may be unavailable

I need to be alone sometimes

- I'm OK with some kissing, but I'm not prepared to engage in sex for now.

It tends to be useful to thoroughly consider your own boundaries, regardless of what your relationship status is. Start by focusing on how you feel about and respond to circumstances around you, regardless of whether, all things considered, on social media or films you watch. What causes you to feel awkward? What's critical to you? What would you like to keep hidden? Is there conduct or characteristic that would not agree with you, ever (at times called a "deal-breaker")? It very well may be useful to record a portion of your thoughts. The word " boundary " can be somewhat deceptive. It means keeping yourself independent. Be that as it may, boundaries are really good at making you independent and free of unnecessary ties.

It is fundamental to have individual boundaries to have healthy relationships. Individual Boundaries are significant on the grounds that they set the essential rules of how you need to be dealt with. Limits are fundamental rules that individuals make to set up how others can carry on around them.,

Would it be advisable for me to go no contact?

There are a few groups of people who will simply not react to or regard boundaries. In that situation, you may decide that the most ideal alternative for your psychological wellness and limits is to go no contact with the person.

Going no contact can be something precarious, and you will need to ensure you have investigated as many different alternatives to going no contact as possible.

A large number of us like to see the positive qualities in our friends and family and figure they could change in the event that they truly needed to, however ultimately, you understand that not every person wants to. Numerous persons are glad to live and putrefy in their own hopelessness since it's a position of solace where they don't have to assume responsibility for their growth. If you discover that an individual continually leaves you depressed, restless, angry, or drained, at that point, it very well may be an ideal opportunity to assess whether you need that individual in your life at all.

Try not to allow others to disgrace you into tolerating their terrible conduct. At the end of the day, you're the one that will have to live with it, so you need to put forth a valiant effort for your personal and emotional wellness.

Regardless of the idea of your relationship, defining boundary is a basic segment to keeping a sound relationship with your partner. Seeking a partner ought not to conflict with your requirements.

Getting one several methods comprehensively knowing yourself, understanding your own and feelings, and having the option to convey them to your life partner adequately.

It is not always clear what your limit issues are and how to share them.

Benefits of setting boundaries

1. Boundaries improve our connections and confidence in ourselves.

Boundaries shield relationships from getting risky. In that manner, they really unite us rather than separate us, and are hence vital in any relationship

Having boundaries permits you to focus on yourself, regardless of whether when you are alone, in your workplace, or in your relationship

2. Boundaries can be adaptable/ flexible

Don't be too rigid with setting your boundaries. It's acceptable to be flexible. Realize that when boundaries are excessively unbending or rigid, problems can happen.

You would prefer not to isolate yourself, dodge closeness inside and out, or surrender all your opportunity to other people. Making boundaries that are too bendy is frequently common for ladies.

3. Boundaries permit us to moderate our enthusiastic energy

Your confidence and character can be affected, and you develop hatred toward others in view of your inability to defend yourself. You don't have to have similar boundaries or comfort levels like everybody. Boundaries that let us have an alternate sweep contingent upon the circumstance or individual can likewise assist you with keeping up the energy to really focus on yourself.

Understand that since you might be glad to assist your closest friend or colleague on moving their load to a different apartment doesn't mean you additionally need to do the weighty enthusiastic lifting when somebody messages about their most recent drama.

Why Boundaries Are Good for You

Not only do personal boundaries support your confidence and reinforce your feeling of personality, they likewise make life much simpler.

Imagine a situation where:

• You don't allow individuals to exploit you.

• You never need to fix others' issues, except if you really need to.

• Nothing anybody does disturbs you.

•You easily overlooked details your family, partner, companions do, and you don't disturb or stress yourself.

•You coolly look on while others become involved with nonsense. Truth be told, you scarcely recall what it seems like to be involved in the rubbish by any stretch of the imagination.

Presently, imagine that situation working out, everyday day after day. Wouldn't you like that? Obviously, you would. Anybody would.

That is the thing that solid good sound boundaries give you.

Good versus poor boundaries

How can you say whether a boundary is good or not? It's critical to perceive that sound boundaries help to assure and protect you; an undesirable boundary looks to control or take advantage of another person. A good boundary could be: "I need space to spend time with my friends and do things I like all alone." But on the off chance that your partner says, "I need you to quit talking with different people/young ladies since you may cheat/I am jealous," that is not a sound boundary; it is a bad sign that your partner may have some trust issues and is attempting to control whom you spend time with.

Can your limits change over time? yes Indeed! It's typical for boundaries to move as we acquire educational experience or get more agreeable in our relationships. We probably won't approve of something toward the start of a relationship; however, we may be thoroughly cool with it a couple of months down the line. Then again, we may understand something crosses a limit for us subsequent to encountering it. Each individual has the privilege to alter their perspective on what their boundaries are whenever it pleases them. What's significant is that you're imparting any limit changes to your partner and you're making changes since YOU need to, not on the grounds that you're being constrained, pressured, or controlled into making them.

You have the right to be protected and regarded, and boundaries have a major impact in making sound relationships that let you be YOU.

Solid healthy boundaries require clear internal limits – knowing your emotions and your duties to yourself as well as other people. Sexual boundaries ensure your comfort level with sexual touch and action – what, where, when, and with whom.

Boundaries are fundamental for sound relationships and, truly, a sound life. Setting and supporting boundaries is a skill. Tragically, it's an ability that a significant number of us don't learn, we may get experience to a great extent through watching others. Be that as it may, for a considerable lot of us, boundary building is a generally new idea and a difficult one.

Having sound boundaries signifies "knowing and understanding what your limits are.

Poor Boundaries and Intimate Relationships

I accept boundary issues are the hardest to manage at the family level. You can generally dump that dumb ass of a sweetheart/friend, a separation is in every case, a call or two away, however, you can never dump your family or parents.

In the event that you have boundary issues in your family, it's feasible you have them in your love life too. What's more, your relationship is the best place to start fixing them.

The truth is that sometimes in your relationship, things were so good and you feel so happy and contented and proud of yourself that you made a good choice with your partner, and then suddenly everything starts going down and you are full of regrets for being involved with such a person.

What's more, there is always fluctuations between the two—fourteen days of happiness, followed by two weeks of hell, followed by a month of joy, ended by a ghastly separation and afterward a sensational divorce. It's a sign of a mutually dependent relationship and as a rule addresses, two individuals unequipped for solid personal boundaries.

My first genuine relationship was this way. At that point, it felt real and I was ecstatic as if it was us against the world. Looking back, it was inconceivably unhealthy and I'm happier not being in it.

Bad Boundaries and Neediness

Individuals need boundaries since they have a significant degree of neediness (or codependence). Individuals who are needy or dependent have an urgent requirement for adoration and fondness from others. To get this adoration and love, they sacrifice their character and remove their limits.

(Unexpectedly, it's the absence of character and boundaries that makes them unattractive to a great many people in any case.)

Individuals who condemn others for their own feelings and actions do so on the grounds that they accept that on the off chance that they put the responsibilities on people around them, they'll get lots of love they've generally needed. On the off chance that they continually paint themselves as a victim, in the end, somebody will come to save them.

Individuals who assume fault for others' feelings and actions are continually hoping to save somebody. They accept that assuming they can "fix" their partner, they will get the affection and appreciation they've generally needed.

Predictably, these two kinds of individuals are attracted unequivocally to each other. Their pathologies match each other impeccably. Also, regularly, they've grown up with parents who each display one of these attributes. So their model for a "cheerful" relationship is one dependent on poor and needy boundaries

Incidentally, the two of them fail totally in addressing each other's requirements. Indeed, the two of them just serve to increase the low esteem and lack of confidence that is holding them back from getting their emotional needs met. The casualty makes an ever-increasing number of issues to address and the saver tackles and settles, however, the affection and appreciation they've generally required are never really communicated to each other.

Individual Boundaries, Self-Esteem, and Identity

Personal boundaries and confidence go together. Individuals with high confidence have solid Personal boundaries What's more, rehearsing sound Personal boundaries is one approach to gather confidence.

Another way is to consider boundary as your personal identity that you cannot do without. At the point when you have these cloudy thoughts regarding your feelings and activities—areas where it's hazy about who is responsible for what, who's to blame, why you're doing what you're doing—you've not built up a strong character for yourself.

For example, in case you're truly into Judo, yet you're continually blaming your instructor for your lack of progress and feel regretful about going to classes on the grounds that your spouse gets lonely when you're not around, at that point you're not possessing that part of your personality. Judo is presently a normal thing for you and not something you are. It becomes inauthentic, another way in the round of getting social approval, instead of to fulfill your own longing to communicate. This is destitution. Furthermore, the reliance on outside approval will drive your confidence lower and make your attitude less appealing.

Emotional boundaries and physical boundaries

Emotional boundaries include isolating your emotions from another person's. Violations include assuming responsibilities for another's emotions, allowing another's sentiments to dictate your own, forfeiting your own needs to satisfy another, reprimanding others for your issues, and accepting responsibilities for another's personal issues.

While physical boundaries refer to your body, privacy, and individual space.

Examples of Personal Boundaries

• Your Entitlement to privacy.

• The Capacity to Adjust Your Perspective.

• Your Entitlement to Your Own Time.

• The Need to Deal with Negative Energy.

• The Opportunity to Communicate Sexual boundaries.

• The Opportunity to Communicate spiritual boundaries.

• The Option to Stay Consistent with Your Standards.

The most effective method to know when you have boundary issues;

- Do you at any point feel like people exploit you or utilize your feelings for their own benefit?
- Do you at any point feel like you're continually having to "save" individuals near you and fix their issues constantly?
- Do you wind up sucked into futile arguments or fighting regularly?
- In your relationships, does it seem like things are in every case either bad or horrible? Or then again maybe you even go through the separation/reunion at regular intervals?
- Do you invest a great deal of energy defending yourself for things you accept aren't your fault?

On the off chance that you addressed "yes" to even a couple of the above mentioned, you most likely define and keep up poor boundaries in your relationships. In the event that you addressed a resounding "yes" to most of the items of the things above, you not just have a significant boundary issue in your relationships, however, you likewise presumably have some other individual issues going on in your life.

Before we proceed to fix those boundary issues, we should discuss what they are first.

Sound Personal Boundaries = Taking responsibility regarding your own behavior and feelings, while NOT taking the responsibility regarding the actions or feelings of others.

Individuals with poor boundaries normally come in two ways: the individuals who assume an excessive amount of liability for the feelings/activities of others and the individuals who anticipate that others should assume a lot of liability for their own feelings/activities.

Strangely, these two sorts of individuals frequently end up together.

A few instances of poor boundaries:

- "You can't go out with your companions without me. You realize how jealous I get. You need to remain at home with me."

- "Sorry folks, I can't go out with you this evening, my sweetheart gets truly furious when I go out without her."
- "My associates are morons and I'm in every case late to gatherings since I need to reveal to them how to take care of their responsibilities."
- "I'd love to take that work in Lagos; however, my mom could never excuse me for moving so distant."
- "I can date you; however, can you not tell my companion Vicky? She gets truly jealous when I have a sweetheart and she doesn't."

In every situation, the individual is either making duty regarding moves/feelings that are not theirs or they are requesting that another person assume liability for their activities/feelings.

Unhealthy boundaries include a disregard for your own and others' important needs and boundaries points.

Since you know a little of the vital kinds of boundaries you may wish to set in your relationship, how would you go about it?

It should not shock you to discover that transparent communication is the way to opening fruitful boundary settings and the regarding of those boundaries.

It's pretty much as straightforward as following these steps.

Step 1 – Know Your Boundaries

Maybe you have discovered inspirations in the above-mentioned points and have some thought of what boundaries you'd prefer to set.

Yet, all things being equal, it merits taking the effort to truly distinguish where you remain on the scope of issues spoken about, and to consider different areas where you have red lines a partner should adhere to.

It is when your boundaries are known to you, that can you impart them to your partner.

Step 2 – Choose When To Discuss Them

A few things should be talked about genuinely from the beginning of a relationship since they may assume a major part in you and your partner's joy and the general soundness of your relationship.

At the point when you feel the opportunity has come to examine a specific boundary, try to do so when you are both free from interruptions and when you can both listen to each other.

Other issues can stand by until they need to be raised.

It's excessive, for example, to state categorically that you won't endure being yelled at until/except if you end up in that situation.

And, after it's all said and done, it is ideal to trust that things will quiet down so you and your partner can chat with less passionate energy to confuse things.

Step 3 – Make your boundaries Clear

In the event that you need your partner to submit to your boundaries, you should make them clear and effectively understood.

There is no place for uncertainty and vague situations if these things truly mean a lot to you.

Get your partner to repeat back what they think your limit is. This will permit you to be certain that they have understood.

While communicating your limits, use "I" proclamations rather than "you" explanations.

So, say:

"I would favor it if your Mother called first prior to coming round."

As opposed to:

"You need to advise your mom to telephone before she comes round."

Step 4 – Allow For Some Minor changes

No one is perfect, people commit errors. While there are some major issues that you essentially won't acknowledge, you need to give your partner some room on the off chance that they forgot a portion of your boundaries especially when you first conveyed them.

Maybe they disregard your desire to be alone for a while so you may rest and re-energize. It's a blameless mistake to make, and they do it since they don't understand your needs.

It's surely not something to make a big noise about, except if they keep on ignoring your emotions on numerous occasions.

Continue to help them to remember your preferences and they should, at last, come to regard and respect them.

Step 5 – Know When And How To Be Insistent

There may come a moment that one of your strict boundaries has been crossed, or your partner may continue to commit little errors or mistakes around things that are somewhat less important to you.

In any case, a time will come when you need to show that there are ramifications to their actions.

On the off chance that you don't, they will keep on overlooking your boundaries and continue taking advantage of you.

For certain things, your partner has to know the results before the main infraction. On the off chance that, for instance, you essentially can't tolerate any type of cheating at all, you need to make it clear consistently that you will cut off the relationship should this happen.

Sometimes, you may have to talk about the consequence of a crossing of a less important boundary.

Thus, for example, if they stay out late with friends without telling you, you can clarify that on the off chance that they do so once more, they will invest more time with your family as a consequence.

Try not to Be Afraid To Revisit Discussions

Individuals change. Relationships change. Boundaries change.

Plainly speaking, sound boundaries unite couples if they know that they can talk honestly to each other without fear of recrimination or unmerited judgment.

At the point when we're ready to see that defining boundaries in a relationship doesn't restrict it however it fortifies it, the adolescent dream that somebody must be open and totally our own offers a route to the more grown-up enthusiasm for our friends and family as people.

Asking and regarding are key segments in any relationship, and actually, we as a whole have limits, we essentially don't generally set out to state them or, now and then, even inspect them. Examining limits shouldn't be viewed as a difficult situation, but instead placing trust and confidence truly enduring longer than an unbounded dream.

CHAPTER TWO

21 Examples of Healthy Boundaries in Relationships

1. Saying No

You may think that it's simpler to forfeit your own personal needs for your partners out of a dread of disturbing them.

Notwithstanding, in the event that they request something from you that conflicts with your standards, wastes your time, or sacrifice something significant, it's all right to say no. you don't have to be harsh, yet figure out how to say it emphatically.

2. Refusal to Take Blame

Once in a while, your partner may accuse you out of hurt or blame. This conduct doesn't mean their anger is your fault. Try not to allow them to skirt obligation by controlling your feelings. Recognize their agony, let them realize you are there for them however affirm that you won't take responsibility regarding their actions.

3. Always expect Respect

You merit respect and loving communication. In the event that you feel your partner is being disrespectful to you and talking out of anger, you are entitled to remove yourself from the scene.

If you must have a discussion, it must be with respect.

4. Dictating Your Own Feelings

When you are a couple, sentiments and feelings can feel obscured. Figure out how to decipher your sentiments from your partner's and their view of your emotions. In the event that they speak for you, right then and there ask that they don't dictate your feelings for you and that you can speak for yourself.

5. Finding Your Identity Outside of the Relationship

Codependency can prompt a merging of personalities. "I" becomes "we," and the "you" lose all sense of direction in the blend. Recollect that you are one portion of entirety as well as your own individual with interests, passions, and lively intelligence. It's OK to have a self-appreciation separate from your partner.

6. Learn to accept Help

Some groups of people are not free and find it hard to depend on their partners in difficult times. If you are one of these groups of people and you need assistance, it very well may be a great idea to set up where your limits are and what you do constantly need or not need assistance with.

You may request assistance with managing funds, however, need space when managing family issues. This equilibrium can be a sensitive tango, however open communication prompts a smoother rhythm.

7. Requesting Space

• In some cases, we simply need alone time from everyone. In a relationship, it can seem like you are never alone. Requesting space may feel to your partner like you are driving him/her away, despite the fact that that is not your aim.

Alone time is highly recommended and a vital aspect for keeping up your own personality and figuring out your issues. On the off chance that you're not clear about requiring space, your partner may feel dismissed or that you're maintaining a strategic distance from them. Mentioning it from the beginning that you like to stay alone sometimes will help later on.

8. Conveying Discomfort

Regardless of whether your partner makes a harmful or dirty joke at your expense or crosses an actual line, figuring out how to explain your distress unmistakably will help in defining your boundaries. Tell them what you won't tolerate, and design a strategy on the off chance that the person crosses that boundary.

9. Mutual Sharing

It's all right to take things slowly at the beginning of a relationship. Try not to feel forced to share everything forthright or feel you need to share first for your loved one to open up. Weakness ought to be common, with the two partners checking in and making a protected space for sharing

10. Standing Up for Yourself

In an argument, you or your partner may make statements you may later regret that are mean or terrible. Ensure it's known that you will not acknowledge the person in question addressing you that way. You have inherent worth and have the right to be addressed in a polite manner. Spread the word about it that you need an apology and that you need your partner to recognize the hurt their words have caused.

11. Deciding to be Vulnerable

Weakness ought not to be requested. Obviously, it is a significant segment of a sound relationship, yet you ought to never feel compelled to open up about a troublesome topic in any stage of your relationship.

You share your emotions and encounters on your own terms. Do not hesitate to let it be known that you need time to discuss any painful topic.

12. Right to Privacy

There are various degrees of privacy. You may share a home PC, however, remain quiet about your email password. This decision is sensible. Your assets, thoughts, messages, diary entries, and even subjects on a past relationship or even marriage, divorce, or traumas are yours to share or not at your own discretion. Encroachment on those limits is not acceptable.

13. The Ability to Change Your Mind at will

Your decisions are your choice, similar to the choice to make another one. In the event that you alter your perspective, your partner ought not to cause you to feel bad for it. Be clear with your thinking or simply states that you chose to alter your decision. Obviously, being open is important, yet it ought to occur on your terms.

14. You Own Your Own Time

You will dictate where and with whom you want to spend your time, alone or separated. Perhaps you hate going to Monday night football. Make it known that Monday evenings are your alone time or your weekly night out with your friends. Maybe you need alone time after a major disagreement; you are within your entitlement to request that.

15. Handling Negative Energy

A personal boundary can likewise be one that you set for your own conduct. It is critical to explore unhealthy anger and disdain so you're not bringing negative energy into your home.

On the off chance that you can't handle it all alone, request help. Offer your toxic feelings and ease up those harmful sentiments by speaking the truth about your mindset.

16. Expressing Sexual Boundaries

The beginnings of actual closeness with a partner is an exciting time, however, exploring personal boundaries in sex can be abnormal or even startling. Transparently conveying your requirements or distresses is fundamental, however finding the words can be precarious.

Recollect that each progression you take requires energetic assent from your partner, and you ought to never feel constrained into anything. Talk with one another routinely. Offer dreams and talk about boundaries. Trustworthiness and vulnerability are amazing.

17. Expressing Spiritual Boundaries

Your convictions are your own, regardless of how much you could conceivably share for all intents and purpose with your partner as far as religion is concerned. You and your life partner should regard each other's convictions, cultivate and energize each other's spiritual development, and be available to find out about the other's way of life or faith.

18. Being able to Remain True to Your Principles

Set a limit with yourself that your standards stay set up regardless of who you are dating. Obviously, you can alter your perspective as your discussions with your partner open new ways to new ideas. Yet, you shouldn't feel constrained to embrace their positions out of dread of disturbing them.

19. The right to Communicate Physical Needs

Figure out how to convey what your body needs. Is it safe to say that you are a veggie lover and don't need meat in the house? Is it accurate to say that you are a go-getter who should be sleeping before 10:00 pm? At that point ensure your partner regards your actual needs by not making boisterous clamors or watching the TV till late into the night and ere by disturbing your sleep.

Then again, find out about your life partner's boundaries. In the event that they incline toward a later sleep time, work out a game plan as opposed to constraining them to rest before their organic clock permits them to.

20. Your Right to Own Material Possessions

Choosing what to share and what to save for yourself is never a simple task. A few couples open joint accounts, while others prefer to handle their finances independently. Material and monetary limits are common in each relationship.

21. Your Time Is Your Own To Manage As You Like

Another relationship boundary to set for yourself is figuring out how to deal with your time in a manner that doesn't disregard your partner.

Here are a couple of tips to assist you with beginning building up boundaries with your partner in your relationship:

• Communicate your thoughts with each other.

• Never undermine your partner's feelings.

• Fulfill your promises.

• Take responsibility for your actions.

• Know when it's an ideal opportunity to proceed onward.

How do you communicate your boundaries?

How might you and your partner know each other's l boundaries? By discussing them! Communication is truly key in a sound relationship, and boundaries are a significant piece of a continuous discussion among you and your partner. Discussing limits can happen at any point, any place! On the off chance that your partner accomplishes something that you like or don't care for, let them know. A straightforward, "Hello, I truly like it when you… " or "I'm not happy when we… "tell them what's up. In a solid relationship, partners regard each other's limits whenever they've been conveyed. What's more, in case you're ever not satisfied with your partner's boundaries, simply ask! Questions like "Is this all right?" or "Are you cool with this?" can help kick off the discussion. Simply recall: on the off chance that you would prefer not to discuss your limits with your partner since you're apprehensive they'll respond with outrage or savagery, that is a red flag that your relationship may be bad or damaging.

Unhealthy boundaries include negligence for your own and others' qualities, needs, and boundary points. Here are a few instances of what undesirable limits may resemble: Disrespecting the qualities, convictions, and assessments of others when you disagree with them. Not saying "no" or not agreeing when others say "no."

The most effective method to Set your boundaries

This is more difficult than one might expect. Yet, you will waste time except if you characterize what your own limits are. What will you endure or not endure in your life? What practices will you acknowledge or not acknowledge? From your family, your spouse, your companions, your partners, your postal carrier, the person higher up, your first date.

Choose what the results are on the off chance that somebody disrupts one of your rules. This will undoubtedly occur, and regularly. What's more, it will be hard to consider what the outcomes ought to be once it does. You'll be one-sided by the individual, the unique situation, and a horde of different elements. So choose wisely.

Impart the above plainly. Spread the word about your boundaries. This is especially significant for individuals nearest to you. It's presumably OK for the delivery guy to not have the foggiest idea about any of your boundaries, however, it's by no means okay for your partner to not realize when they've gone too far. On the off chance that somebody crosses your limits, do what you said you would. Be humane, however, be firm.

Limits and Sacrifice

The greatest counter-contention to executing exacting personal boundaries, or defense, based upon your viewpoint, is that occasionally you need to make sacrifices for your loved ones. In the event that your better half/sweetheart has an irrational requirement for you to call/ text them regularly or daily, regardless of whether it's simply to talk for three minutes, at that point, it could be sensible to fulfill a little sacrifice to make them happy with you.

However, here's the trick:

In the event that you make a sacrifice for somebody you care about, it should be on the grounds that you need to, not on the grounds that you feel pressure or on the grounds that you dread the outcomes of not doing it.

It means that demonstrations of fondness and affections are only valid on the off chance that they're performed without assumptions.

But peradventure that you call your spouse every day and you hate doing it and feel like they're obstructing on your independence and you loathe them and you're frightened by how angry they'll be assuming you don't call; you have a boundary issue. Assuming you do it since you love them and wouldn't fret, do it.

It tends to be hard for individuals to perceive whether they're accomplishing something out of apparent commitment or out of deliberate sacrifice. Here's simply the litmus test: ask, "In the event that I quit doing this, how might the relationship change?" If you're truly terrified of the changes, that is an awful sign. On the off chance that the results are horrible, however, you have a feeling that you could quit playing out the action without feeling bad about yourself, at that point, that is a decent sign.

The explanation is that assuming there's a boundary issue, you will fear the deficiency of that cross-responsibility regarding each other. On the off chance that there's not a boundary issue, i.e., you're doing it as a favor without expectations, at that point, you're OK with the repercussions of not doing it. An individual with sound boundaries isn't apprehensive about a fit, argument, or getting injured. An individual with weak boundaries is frightened by it.

An individual with sound boundaries understands that it's absurd to anticipate that two people should oblige each other 100% and satisfy each need the other has. An individual with solid limits understands that they may offend someone in some cases, at the end of the day they can't decide how others feel. An individual with solid limits comprehends that a sound relationship isn't controlling each other's feelings, yet rather each partner supporting each other in their growth and way to self-realization. There are some questions you need to ask yourself when somebody will not regard your boundaries.

Are the boundaries sensible? Does it regard the other person's boundaries?

It's generally regular for people to over-correct when they are attempting to work through their issues and challenges that they are facing. You may find that you set unhealthy boundaries for them to follow as a result of the fact that you have battled with boundary issues previously.

The most ideal approach to decide if your boundary is sensible is by listening in to the person you are having issues with. Assuming they can explain what issue, they are having with the boundary, you can decide if your boundary is reasonable and important.

Boundaries are not generally something firm. Now and then, there are exemptions to the guidelines. You may track down that a boundary you raised doesn't serve you in the manner that you figured it did or that it is excessively restrictive.

You may end up needing to adjust your boundaries when you've developed more feelings with a person or need to give them a chance for the relationship to flourish.

It's additionally conceivable that you may have some underlying clash with a person as you both attempt to track down and measure where your separate boundaries are.

You will need to take some time and truly consider which of your limits are adaptable and which are definitely not. There are a few sorts of limits and convictions that a person just can't be adaptable with. It very well may be something they find ethically wrong, feel is frightful to them, or they recently concluded that this specific limit isn't adaptable.

A genuine example would be cheating in a relationship. A few persons may decide to remain and work it out, to fix whatever broke and protect the relationship. What's more, others quickly cut off the association and leave, as they see cheating as a huge break of trust and regard that they can't endure or excuse it.

Neither one of the choices isn't right. Everything relies upon the individual with the boundary and how adaptable they decide to be with it. It's all right if the individual chooses to attempt to work it out. It's additionally all right if the individual decides to cut off of the association, and there's nothing left to do except for leave.

Consider how flexible the limit is that is being pushed. Is there a chance for flexibility to build the relationship? Or on the other hand is it something you believe you should stand firm on?

Would it be advisable for you to part from the person?

Assuming your boundaries are sensible, that it isn't flexible, and the person is still going against them, then you need to settle on a decision on how to engage with this person.

You may find that their overall conduct isn't healthy or fitting and pull away totally. You may likewise find that despite the fact that you need to do that, you're not ready to because of different responsibilities or attachments, or the person is a colleague or a relative who will turn others against you.

Separating can be a preferable decision over going no contact if the circumstance doesn't warrant it, or if going no contact is not feasible.

Ways to separate include:

1. Keep all discussions simply business – no more easygoing discussion with the person, just be polite

2. Try not to spend an unnecessary amount of time with the person that you don't need to.

3. Try not to be disrespectful. They may simply be attempting to get you furious, so they have the motivation to collaborate with others or give them ammo to paint you in a negative light.

4. Stay quiet or leave casual discussions. Do not accept their calls and don't call them either.

Keep in mind, you can't handle the actions of others. Your boundaries will help illuminate and control them, however. In the event that you don't stick around to endure their nonsense, they will ultimately get the message that you won't endure having your boundaries disregarded.

You may think that its supportive to foreordain how long you will give the individual in the event that you need to separate.

Half an hour in length call may not be too stressful, however on the off chance that it goes a lot further or become rude, it's all right to end it. Restricting time can help situations where you can't or don't have any desire to go full no contact.

CHAPTER THREE

The most effective method to construct your very own and emotional space

Our own limits aren't pretty much as clear as a fence or a goliath with a "no access" sign, regrettably, they're more similar to undetectable air pockets.

Despite the fact that personal boundaries can be trying to explore, setting and conveying them is fundamental for our wellbeing, prosperity, and surprisingly our security.

We can define boundaries for our;

• personal space

• sexuality

• emotions and feelings

• stuff or assets

• time and energy

• culture, religion, and morals

Defining boundaries for yourself and respecting the boundaries of others is definitely not rocket science, yet you can learn approaches to assume responsibility for your life. Regardless of whether you need to set more clear rules with your family or declare your stand with regards to strangers, here's the manner by which to begin.

9 Different ways to set boundaries with Troublesome Relatives

Most often, people that are the hardest to set boundaries with are people to whom you are the nearest. Regardless of whether your family is a happy one or not, there may in any case be persons from that family that regularly go too far or that just treat you in such a way that you would not really like to be treated. Some people will assume the part of the accommodating person with their families, but there are those your relatives that are being troublesome and that is cutting into your disturbing, it's time to set boundaries for those troublesome relatives. Here are nine different ways to do precisely that:

1.Understand that your requirements are important.

Normally, people will try not to build boundaries out of fear of hurting others, in spite of the way that the other person doesn't seem to allow them a similar graciousness. This is particularly true for troublesome relatives, yet it is essential to remember that your necessities are similarly pretty much as important as the next person's requirements. This is a sort of manipulation, to cause you to feel like you can't set up boundaries in light because their requirements are more important than yours.

2. Search out people who regard you.

In the event that there are your relatives that do truly love you, search them out and use them to help you set boundaries with the relatives that don't appear to regard you. If there are no such persons from your family who can assist you with this, look for people outside the circle of your family. Your group of friends is a decent place to search. You will undoubtedly have at any rate one friend that can help you begin to build the boundaries that you need.

3. Be firm, however kind.

Defining boundaries don't really mean you must be hard. Indeed, when you build your limits with those troublesome relatives, it can really be more effective to do it with thoughtfulness. Outrage or protectiveness will just aggravate them up and cause them to lash out at you. Consideration, be that as it may, prompts a more noteworthy probability of a calm exchange.

4. Keep your expectations reasonable.

For instance, it isn't reasonable to consent to go to Thanksgiving at a family member's home, when you realize that they will disparage you the whole time that you are there. Yielding and going to family occasions or effectively searching out situations in which you and that family member are together is something contrary to defining and keeping boundaries. Be practical with by not spending time with negative people.

5. Leave.

Something that the vast majority neglect is that in the event that somebody is being poisonous, you do have the choice to get up and leave the situation. You may feel like you need to guard yourself, however on the off chance that your troublesome relatives are specialists at making you appear as though the miscreant or causing you to feel terrible for exploding after they have been poisonous to you for quite a long time, the best thing to do is just leave. Simply get moving. You don't need to explain for yourself to anybody; you don't need to apologize.

6. Remember that you are accountable for what you do.

Nobody else can cause you to do or to feel anything. You are responsible for whether you keep up your boundaries. For instance, say that you are at a family gathering and your troublesome uncle says something painful about your work. At the point when you advise him to quit ridiculing you, he says something regarding how you've never been good at taking a joke. At this moment, you have two options. You can either imagine that all is great or you can say something like, "That is going too far. In case you continue, I'm simply going to leave." This sets up what is and what isn't OK and returns the results of the action on the troublesome uncle.

7. Be Honest.

Dropping clues or being inactively forceful about your boundaries is the most noticeably terrible approach to ensure that anybody understands what they are, particularly in light of the fact that numerous troublesome relatives are troublesome explicitly on the grounds that they are imprudent. Being extremely direct and honest about what is OK and what isn't OK is the best and only way you can ensure that they understand what your limits are.

8. Make yourself number one priority.

At the point when you make yourself number one priority, you are exceptionally able to set up and adhere to your boundaries. Self-care can assist you with understanding the significance of your own limits and can likewise assist with inspiring you to ensure your limits are characterized and that they are being noticed. While putting yourself first all the time isn't healthy, every so often set aside the effort to think often about yourself above all else, particularly when managing troublesome relatives is vital.

9. Figure out how to be decisive.

Numerous troublesome individuals pull off being troublesome on the grounds that nobody confronts them. Regardless of whether your dad appears to appreciate bringing you down or your cousins' teasing regularly crosses a line and goes excessively far, basically being self-assured and mentioning to individuals what you need can be sufficient to define the boundaries you need. On the off chance that you are confident, you become somebody that individuals don't fool with, somebody that is regarded, as opposed to criticizing. Stand up for yourself!

7 Ways to Set Boundaries With Narcissistic People

1. Don't defend, clarify, or justify yourself.

2. Leave when it doesn't feel all right with you.

3. Decide what you will endure and what you will not.

4. Learn to cunningly evade meddlesome inquiries or negative remarks.

5. Take the domineering jerk by the horns. ...

6. Don't belittle the force of narcissism. ...

7. Remember: Good boundaries bring good results.

Ways To Deal With Someone Who Repeatedly Disrespects Your Boundaries

There are a couple of inquiries you need to pose to yourself when somebody will not regard your limits.

Is the limit sensible? Does it regard the other individual's limits?

It's moderately regular for individuals to over-right when they are attempting to work through their private matters. You may find that you set unhealthy boundaries because you have battled with boundaries in your previous relationship.

• Take yourself out of the equation.

• Don't fall into their snare.

• Don't use obscure language.

• Don't surrender.

- Don't show them that you feel bad about any situation.

- Set a standard and stick to it.

- Remain calm in every way possible.

Great personal boundaries protect you. Having a feeling of boundaries and cutoff points likewise assists you with associating with your real self. They depend on your convictions, beliefs, emotions, choices, decisions, needs, requirements, and decisions. They are clear, firm, and sometimes changeable.

Get expert help managing somebody who disregards your limits.

People don't generally work hard at respecting people's limits. At times it's deliberate, sometimes it's definitely not.

In some cases, your expectations may not be in accordance with what others are willing to oblige. You have the last say on what you are willing or not willing to accept.

Be that as it may, on the off chance that you have a considerable long list of necessities on how you hope to be treated or dealt with or change those lists every now and again, you ought to anticipate that people would not be able to keep up, so they quit or stop being mindful of your boundaries. People don't generally work effectively at regarding personal boundaries. Some of the time it's malevolent, once in a while, it's definitely not.

That goes too far from a sound sense of pride and boundaries to simply being high-maintenance and manipulative.

5 Different ways to React to People Who Abuse Your Limits.

• Ensure your boundaries are clear to yourself and to others, it should not be vague

• You're in Control Here, Act Like It

• Keep a record of any violations of your boundaries for any adjustments.

• Accept That Not Every Person Will Regard Your Limits.

• Stay away from people who don't respect your boundaries

People who need sound boundaries are most often emotionally needy). They often don't know their worth and are desperate for adoration and approval from others. Fed up, they lash out of resentment or fits of remorse, reprimanding others for their emotional misery.

Indeed, defining boundaries can be awkward, particularly in the event that you've never done it.

You protect yourself by defining boundaries.

Stage 1: Pray without ceasing.

Stage 2: Know your needs.

Stage 3: Be straightforward and clear about your needs.

Stage 4: Have your consequences prepared, and use them!

Stage 5: Get support.

Setting boundaries is realizing what is going and not going right to ensure you are emotionally protected and psychologically okay. Defining boundaries may look like to others that you are being narrow-minded, as they might be under the feeling that you ought to be accessible to them at whatever point you need it.

4 Essential Tips

1. Always ask questions. Clear communication is fundamental for understanding what the other individual's boundaries are.

2. Acknowledge what the other individual is communicating.

3. Regard the self-rule of others.

4. Keep on working on improving yourself.

CHAPTER FOUR

Step by step instructions to Set Boundaries in Relationships

How will you set boundaries in your relationship?

The soundness of your communication characterizes sound relationships.

Understanding your partner's limits will change your capacity to communicate and help stop issues from the beginning before they overwhelm you.

Sound boundaries are an impression of your standards, rules, and guidelines that you have set for yourself. A break in those limits emerges when your partner disregards, overlooks, or doesn't know about those standards or personal requirements.

Having an absence of boundaries can regularly prompt emotional blackmail from your loved one, regardless of whether it's deliberate or not. You may have issues with saying no when somebody asks you for some help, or you may despise public display of friendship.

Provided that this is true, you should make speak out those needs to your partner.

Figure out how to perceive the signs that somebody has crossed your limits. These include feelings of outrage, disdain, or blame.

The discussion you have with our accomplice might be extreme from the outset, however, it very well may be the way into a happy relationship.

There are numerous types of boundaries in a relationship and marriage, that can set up better and lasting communication and closeness.

Some discussions might be easier than others, however, it's better they happen before an argument as opposed to during the strained minutes after a contention.

It is also advisable to enroll a personal therapist or a couple's advisor to perceive where or when you may need them.

We've made a relationship boundary list to help you with Step-by-step instructions to Set Healthy Boundaries

Poor boundaries are quite often an impression of low confidence (and the other way around), and something should be done to address the one for the other to improve. We should begin with confidence.

To build confidence, you need to understand that it's just the side-effect of being an equipped, balanced person. Confidence isn't something that you seek after for the well-being of its own. Doing that isn't just pointless—it's poisonous.

Confidence is the way you believe you're doing in your life, compared with how every other person is getting along. In the event that you have low confidence, no doubt you're not doing admirably by some measurement or other. Also, the main thing you can do is to practice compassion for yourself.

Nobody is perfect. Try not to be so hard on yourself. Acknowledge your imperfections and figure out how to be OK with them, at that point work on getting better.

It's by tolerating yourself as you are, and afterward dealing with yourself that you can grow your confidence. This is difficult work, and it requires significant investment. However, you'll end up in a far more pleasant spot than you are in at the beginning.

As you come to feel higher regard for yourself, sound boundaries will gradually arise in your life. You will naturally understand what you will or won't tolerate from others, you will take a stand and stand by it, and eliminate yourself from poisonous relationships.

Be that as it may, if this doesn't occur for you normally, or in case you're not exactly there yet with the confidence, here are steps.

The following, are keys to building better boundaries and maintaining them

1. Name your boundaries.

You can't define great limits on the off chance that you're uncertain of where you stand. In this way, distinguish your physical, passionate, mental, and spiritual boundaries, consider what you can endure and acknowledge and what causes you to feel awkward or focused. Those emotions assist us with recognizing what our cutoff points are.

2. Tune into your emotions.

I have noticed two key emotions in others that are warnings or signs that we're losing our boundaries: inconvenience and hatred. I proposed thinking about these sentiments on a continuum from one to 10. Six to 10 is in the higher zone

In case you're at the higher finish of this continuum, during communication or in a circumstance, I recommend asking yourself, what is causing that? What is it about this relationship or the person's assumption that is disturbing me?

Disdain normally "comes from being exploited or not appreciated." It's frequently a sign that we're propelling ourselves either past our own cutoff points since we feel remorseful, or another person is forcing their assumptions, perspectives, or values on us. At the point when somebody behaves in a way that causes you to feel awkward, that is a prompt to us that they might be abusing or crossing a limit.

3. Be straightforward.

For certain individuals, keeping up sound boundaries doesn't need an immediate and obvious discourse. Typically, this is the situation if individuals are comparable in their communicating styles, perspectives, characters, and general way to deal with life, they'll approach each other accordingly.

With others, for example, the individuals who have a different character or social background, you'll be more straightforward about your limits. Think about this example: "one individual feels [that] testing somebody's idea is a solid method of communication," yet to someone else this feels distasteful and stressful.

There are times you need to be straightforward. For example, in a romantic relationship, time can turn into a boundary issue. Partners may have to discuss how long they need to spend separately and how long to spend together.

4. Give yourself authorization.

Dread, blame, and self-question are big possible traps. We may fear the other person's reaction if we define and authorize our boundaries. We may feel regret by shouting out or denying a family member. Many accept that they ought to have the option to adapt to a circumstance or say yes since they're a good child, despite the fact that they "feel depleted or exploited." We may doubt whether we even have the right to have boundaries at all.

Boundaries are not the only indication of a sound relationship; they're an indication of confidence and self-respect. Thus, give yourself the permission to define boundaries and work to save them.

5. Ensure self-awareness.

Once more, boundaries are tied in with focusing on your sentiments and respecting them. If you notice yourself slipping and not supporting your boundaries, I recommend asking yourself: What's changed? Consider "What I'm doing or [what is] the other partner/person doing?" or "What is the circumstance evoking that is making me angry or pushed?" At that point, think about your choices: "What do I do about the situation? What do I have command over?"

6. Think about your past and present.

How you were raised alongside your responsibilities in your family can turn into extra snags in defining and safeguarding boundaries. If you are the firstborn that take care of your younger siblings, you figured out how to focus on others, leaving your needs last. Overlooking your own needs may have become the standard for you.

Likewise, consider people you surround yourself with, "Is there love on both sides?" Is there a sound give and take?

7. Focus on self-care.

I help my customers focus on self-care, which likewise includes allowing them to put themselves first. At the point when we do this, our need and inspiration to define boundaries become more defined. Self-care additionally implies perceiving the importance of your emotions and respecting them. These sentiments fill in as significant prompts about our prosperity and about what makes us glad and sad.

Putting yourself first additionally gives you the energy, genuine feelings of serenity, and inspirational viewpoint to be more present with others and be there for them.

Also, when we're in a better spot, we can be better spouse, mother, husband, colleague, or friend.

8. Look for help.

In case you're struggling with boundaries, look for some help, regardless of whether at a care group, church, directing, training or old buddies. With friends or family, you can even focus on it with one another to work on defining boundaries together and hold each other accountable.

Consider looking for help through resources too by reading books in that niche.

9. Be confident.

Obviously, we realize that it's insufficient to have boundaries; we really need to ensure we follow it. Despite the fact that we realize mentally that people aren't mind readers, we actually anticipate that others should understand what hurts us. Since they don't, it's essential to confidently speak with the other person when they've crossed a boundary.

In a deferential manner, let the other person know what specifically is disturbing to you and that you can join hands together to address it.

10. Start gradually.

Like any new expertise, decisively imparting your boundaries takes practice. I recommend beginning with a little boundary that isn't threatening to you and afterward gradually expanding to additional difficult boundaries. Expand upon your success first and do whatever it takes not to take on something that feels overwhelming. Introduction to boundaries

CHAPTER FIVE

Boundaries in marriage

Would it be advisable for you to have limits in marriage?

100% yes. All relationships require boundaries for optimal success and wellbeing.

While the word boundaries can sound somewhat scary, they really fill a significant need in a marriage or relationship. Undoubtedly, boundaries ought to be available in the entirety of our relational connections, not simply our heartfelt ones.

What's more, as we'll before long discover, boundaries are not simply significant, they really will fortify and improve a marriage.

Indeed, even in the union of marriage, wherein two are said to be one, there is still a significant requirement for boundaries. Allow us to investigate what those may be, and how to create them in your own marriage.

5 Significant boundaries in marriage

The limits you create in your marriage are probably going to differ broadly dependent on your own characters, needs, and situation as a couple. It's likewise critical to take note that boundaries can be fluid, changing and adjusting as the case may be.

Most importantly, the main reason for building and keeping up sound boundaries is to impart about them obviously and regularly. Discuss often what you need in your marriage. Talk about your expectations. Be exceptionally clear on what you will and won't endure from a partner. Tune in to what your spouse needs and hear how you can regard their boundaries. This is probably going to be a continuous process for the duration of the existence of your marriage.

Privacy

Privacy might be probably the most straightforward limit to understand. We as a whole need and merit our personal privacy. So how would you guarantee that privacy is regarded and accessible to the two partners? By defining boundaries around privacy matters.

What does privacy resemble in your relationship? Do you figure couples should share everything? Do you value honesty above all else?

Some people are normally more private than others

On a more unmistakable level, privacy for some, couples include passwording their phones and social media accounts.

Will you two exchange passwords? Does your spouse have access to your social media accounts and emails?

These can be exceptionally close-to-home worries that should be discussed as a team. Talk about what privacy means to you, and how you can get an answer that suits both of you.

Social media: one of the limits you may have to talk about as a couple

Note that this is one area in which boundaries can undoubtedly be bridged. For example, if your partner offers you open access to their telephone and messages, that is incredible. yet, it doesn't give you permission to dive into their inbox continually. This can be a significant violating of limits, and such conduct demonstrates different issues, similar to an absence of trust in your relationship, or a need to control.

Then again, if your partner's boundary includes giving you limited access to their phones and emails, you should get used to it and respect that. You can deal with this boundary in a manner that fulfills you both and doesn't prompt doubt and distrustfulness. In the event that you suffer insecurity and want to follow all your partner's moves, this boundary is probably going to be hard for you. Be that as it may, once more, this conduct is obviously highlighting a more serious issue. As usual, clear and open communication is everything.

Time

Boundaries in regards to time are equally very important.

Time is an important product, and along these lines, we would prefer not to squander our own—or our partner's. Be that as it may, respecting time frequently implies deciding explicit boundaries. Always respect each other's work time and alone time

Space (Physical and Passionate)

Space is a boundary that is firmly identified with time and to privacy, from various perspectives. At the point when you respect your spouse's time, you frequently all the while regarding his space and his security.

Yet, space can likewise mean more than permitting your life partner to be truly far off from you, [when your spouse isn't feeling cuddly, do not hang all over him]

Emotional space implies permitting your partner to have their own sentiments, feelings, and reactions. It implies tolerating how they react to things, in any event, when you don't understand it or like it. At the point when your partner is angry, it implies giving them the opportunity to measure and manage their feelings how they see fit. It implies offering support, however doing whatever it takes not to bounce in and tackle things.

This one can be trying for us all. You may have heard before that men will in general be more "solution bound" than ladies. This can bring about a spouse looking to assist his better half with passionate issues by proposing suggestions and the most proficient method to fix it. In some cases, however, what your partner needs isn't a solution. At such critical points in time, give them the space to be separated from everyone else, alone time with their thoughts, with you simply holding them and listening to them.

Not certain what they need at the time? Simply inquire.

This kind of space is essential in conflict situations, as well. To protect each other's limits, we should endeavor not to discredit each other's feelings. All things being equal, account for these feelings. Leave them alone there and don't invalidate them.

Sexuality

Sexuality requests boundaries also.

In marriage, sex is a blessing; an outflow of the most profound love and yearning for your spouse.

Be that as it may, your spouse isn't there to be your sex toy. It's not sex-on-request in a marriage, getting it when you need it without your partner's say.

While sex is the meeting up of two individuals, the merging of two people into one, there are as yet close to home limits that should be kept up and that should be discussed.

Boundaries to examine with your partner likes in bed include things like: what you are agreeable or not happy with in bed? How regularly would you say you are free for sex? What frequency is fulfilling for you? How might you oversee differences in sex drive, if there are any?

Sexual boundaries guarantee that your sexual coexistence prospers all together, and is important and enjoyable for both of you.

Friends and Outside Influences

Some of the time, boundaries are to shield us from others, yet to shield us from ourselves, or from things that could harm our relationship. Probably the best example is by the way you explore friendship with others, especially with the opposite sex.

Make certain to discuss this with your spouse. What is important in regards to associating with friends outside the home? One thing to talk about is friendships/social time in general. Friendships are so significant in our lives, and they give an important source of help and support that is not quite the same as what our spouse gives us.

Be that as it may, what are your social boundaries? Do you have to inform your spouse prior to going out with friends? Do the details of your friends have to be "shared" or would you say you are cool with having some different friends?

A particularly significant point to examine is friendship with persons from the opposite sex. Many people have solid sentiments about this, so be certain you and your partner know (and regard) each other's limits in this space.

As I would like to think, friendship from the other gender is fine, however, there are limits. I wouldn't need my significant other routinely messaging or informing another lady, or dining out with her alone, and so forth Obviously, there are special cases, especially for mutual friends or those I know well, however, I figure it very well may be critical to have a limit of not permitting yourself to get into possible arguments with a person from the opposite sex.

CHAPTER SIX

CONCLUSION

How would you stop codependency and set limits?

Identify patterns in your daily existence. Whenever you have an idea about what codependency really resembles, take a step back and attempt to recognize any repetitive examples in your current and past relationships.

- Set limits for yourself.

- Keep in mind, you can just control your own behavior.

- Offer solid help

Defining boundaries takes boldness, practice, and support. What's more, remember that it's an expertise you can dominate.

To begin sorting your boundaries out, attempt these four things.

- Know your cutoff points. Clearly characterize what your intellectual, emotional, enthusiastic, physical, and spiritual boundaries are with outsiders, work associates, companions, family, and friends.

- Be self-assured.

- Practice makes perfect.

• If all else fails, move on.